FOOTBALL FOCUS
RULES OF THE GAME

21

Clive Gifford

WAYLAND

First published in 2009 by Wayland

Copyright © Wayland 2009

This paperback edition first published
by Wayland in 2012

Wayland
Hachette Children's Books
338 Euston Road
London NW1 3BH

Wayland Australia
Level 17/207 Kent Street
Sydney, NSW 2000

Editor: Julia Adams
Produced by Tall Tree Ltd
Editor, Tall Tree: Jon Richards
Designer: Ben Ruocco

British Library Cataloguing in Publication Data

Gifford, Clive.
    Rules of the game. -- (Football focus)
    1. Soccer--Rules--Juvenile literature.
    I. Title II. Series
    796.3'3402022-dc22

ISBN 9780750267533

Printed in China

Wayland is a division of Hachette Children's Books, an
Hachette UK company.

www.hachette.co.uk

Acknowledgements
The author and publisher would like to thank the
following people for their help and participation in this
book: Whiteknights FC, Eric Burrow, Steve Rendell and
Paul Scholey

Picture credits
All photographs taken by Michael Wicks, except;
t - top, l - left, r - right, b - bottom, c - centre
cover t - Dreamstime.com/Jimsphotos, tr - Dreamstime.com/
Photosfromafrica, br - Dreamstime.com/Ivz, bl - Dreamstime.
com/Ivz, tl - Dreamstime.com/Rcyoung, c - Dreamstime.com/
Lariotus, 1 Dreamstime.com/Dong Hj, 4 Dreamstime.com/Ivan
Tykhyi, 5 Dreamstime.com/Daniele Morra, 6 istockphoto.
com/Duncan Walker, 7t Dreamstime.com/Shariff Che' Lah, 7b
Dreamstime.com/Dmitry Argunov, 8 Dreamstime.com/Duncan
Walker, 10 Dreamstime.com/Ivan Tykhyi, 12 Dreamstime.com/
Steve Woods, 13b Dreamstime.com/Ami Levin, 15 Dreamstime.
com/Igor Zhorov, 17b Dreamstime.com/Matt Trommer, 18
Dreamstime.com/Lario Tus, 20 Dreamstime.com/Mitchell
Gunn, 21 Andres Stapff/Reuters/Corbis, 22 Sampics/Corbis, 23
Dreamstime.com/Dong Hj, 29 Srdjan Suki/epa/Corbis, 30 Rafael
Diaz/epa/Corbis, 32 Dreamstime.com/Ivan Tykhyi

CONTENTS

The game's laws

Football is an exciting and dynamic team ball sport. The game is played according to a set of rules, or laws, that are reviewed regularly by the sport's governing bodies.

Why does football need laws?

Without laws to tell players how to play, football could turn into a chaotic and dangerous game. The laws were created to protect the players from risky play and to make the game exciting to take part in. They also help to make the game fun to watch so that people keep coming to support teams at stadiums around the world and watch games on television.

Ismaël Bangoura (in white) of Guinea shoots at goal while playing for Ukrainian side Dynamo Kiev against English club Arsenal. Players score goals by putting the ball into the opposing team's net using any part of their body, except for their hands and arms.

Laws of the game

Football's key laws are collected together in a booklet called *Laws of the Game*. In total, there are 17 laws in the booklet and these cover all aspects of the game, from the size of the pitch to the players' equipment and from misconduct to the methods of scoring goals.
A team of officials on the pitch oversees matches and makes sure that players follow these laws.

A goalkeeper stretches up to catch a high ball. Law 3 from *Laws of the Game* states that the teams playing a match should contain a minimum of seven players and a maximum of 11, one of whom should be a goalkeeper. The goalkeeper is the only player who can handle the ball on the pitch.

Early rules

More than 150 years ago, football was a rough game similar to rugby, with players grabbing and pulling each other as they tussled for the ball. The first rules were drawn up in the mid-nineteenth century by teams from British public schools and universities.

Rule changes

Members of many early British football teams met in London in 1863 to form the Football Association and draw up a set of rules. Over time, these became *Laws of the Game.* The rules were quite basic at first. Until 1891, many football matches were played without a crossbar on top of the goal posts. Until 1913, goalkeepers were allowed to grab the ball anywhere in their own half of the pitch.

ON THE BALL

In the early days, each English school had its own rules. At Harrow School, for example, a drawn game was replayed the following day with the goals made twice as wide!

These English schoolboys are wearing caps and heavy boots to play football in around 1900. According to the original laws of 1863, players were not allowed to wear boots with metal plates or nails that stuck out from the soles.

Versions of the game

While today's laws deal with the full version of football, there are many different versions of football that are played under their own rules. These include futsal, which is played by teams made up of just five players on an indoor pitch that is smaller than a full-size football pitch. The goal is also smaller, measuring just two metres high by three metres wide.

Russian team VIZ-Sinara (in white) scores a goal against Luparense (in blue) from Italy during a futsal match. As well as having fewer players and a smaller pitch, futsal is played with a lighter and smaller ball than in the full version of the game.

A player is carried off on a stretcher during a match between China and Myanmar. Today, a substitute can take the injured player's place, but this was not allowed before the 1950s. Before this, the injured player's team would play on with just ten footballers.

The law makers

Football's laws are regularly altered and new rules are talked about and tested. Any new law has to be approved by the International Football Association Board (IFAB).

Making the laws

The IFAB is made up of eight representatives – four from FIFA and one from each of the UK's football associations (England, Scotland, Northern Ireland and Wales). The board meets twice a year to study and vote on any law changes. Each representative has one vote and law changes are passed only if they win at least six votes.

Natasha Kai (in white) of the United States celebrates scoring against Canada. She makes sure that she does not get too carried away with her celebration so that she is not punished by the referee.

Modern law changes

The IFAB changes laws in order to make the game safer for players and more exciting for people to watch. For example, the backpass rule was introduced in 1992 and was designed to reduce time-wasting. It means that a goalkeeper cannot handle the ball when it is passed back deliberately by a team-mate. Instead, the goalkeeper must kick or head the ball. In the 1990s and 2000s, players scoring a goal often made elaborate goal celebrations. Referees will now caution any player who is guilty of time-wasting when celebrating a goal. Andres Iniesta scored the winning goal at the 2010 World Cup Final, but because he removed his shirt as he celebrated, he was shown a yellow card by referee, Howard Webb.

RULE SCHOOL
When the referee signals a foul against your team, do not argue or hold onto the ball or you might be cautioned for dissent (arguing) or time-wasting. Run back into position to help your team defend.

This goalkeeper is hurrying to kick the ball clear after a pass from a team-mate. Before the 1992 law change concerning the backpass, she could have picked the ball up, but since this has now been banned, an attacker (shown here in blue) can rush in to challenge the keeper, hoping to force a mistake.

The law enforcers

Major football matches are run by four officials. The referee has ultimate control over the game. There are also two assistants who run the touchlines and the fourth official who helps with several duties.

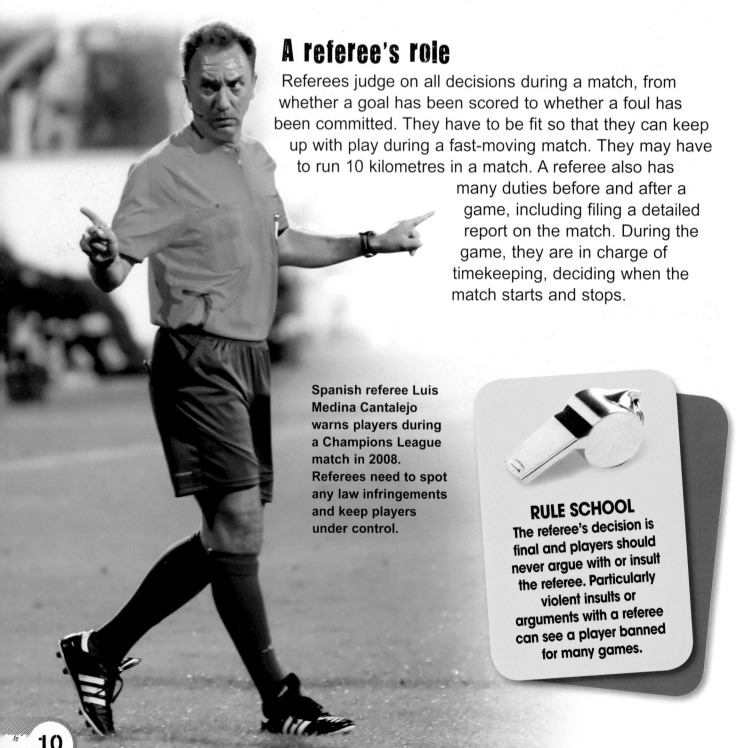

A referee's role

Referees judge on all decisions during a match, from whether a goal has been scored to whether a foul has been committed. They have to be fit so that they can keep up with play during a fast-moving match. They may have to run 10 kilometres in a match. A referee also has many duties before and after a game, including filing a detailed report on the match. During the game, they are in charge of timekeeping, deciding when the match starts and stops.

Spanish referee Luis Medina Cantalejo warns players during a Champions League match in 2008. Referees need to spot any law infringements and keep players under control.

RULE SCHOOL
The referee's decision is final and players should never argue with or insult the referee. Particularly violent insults or arguments with a referee can see a player banned for many games.

Referee's signals

This is the signal for an indirect free-kick. Players who are awarded an indirect free-kick cannot shoot directly at goal, but must pass to a team-mate first.

This is the signal for a direct free-kick. Players who are awarded a direct free-kick can shoot directly at goal.

This referee has awarded a penalty for a serious offence or foul that has taken place inside the penalty area. He is pointing directly at the penalty spot.

Other officials

The referee is helped by a pair of assistants who run each sideline and signal when the ball goes out of play. Assistant referees signal when offside occurs, or when a team wants to make a substitution. They can also advise the referee about a serious foul when the referee does not have a good view. Assistant referees carry flags that they use to communicate with the referee. The fourth official is also on the sidelines, assisting the referee with certain tasks. These include holding up a sign to show how much time is added on at the end of a match, looking after replacement balls and helping when a substitute is made. They can also take the place of an injured official.

> " *I know I have to be good as others may get a chance. It is not easy because I am judged more harshly than a man, and any mistakes are attributed solely to the fact that I am a woman.* "
>
> **Nicole Petignat**, the first female referee of a men's Union of European Football Associations (UEFA) match

Players and pitch

Before a match starts, the referee and assistants check the pitch, goals, balls and the players' kit to make sure that they follow the laws of the game.

Player clothing

Footballers wear a team strip consisting of shirt, shorts, socks, shinpads and, usually, football boots that feature moulded or screw-in studs in the soles for grip. Apart from the goalkeeper, all players in a team must wear the same strip. In a match, the two teams' clothing must be different, to distinguish one team from the other.

RULE SCHOOL
Never wear jewellery or any other items that could be considered dangerous to other players. If a referee spots such an item, they will order you to take it off.

Modern football boots feature moulded plastic studs or screw-in studs made from plastic and metal. Before each match, referees check the players' studs to make sure that there are no sharp edges.

The pitch and playing conditions

The length and width of a full-sized football pitch can vary, but the positions and sizes of the pitch markings are fixed. For example, the penalty area is always 40.3 metres wide and 16.5 metres deep. The penalty spot is 11 metres from the goal line and the centre circle has a diameter of 18.3 metres. The referee is in charge of deciding whether or not a game can start or continue. When the pitch is flooded or frozen, weather conditions are particularly bad or there is serious crowd trouble, the referee can choose to abandon a game.

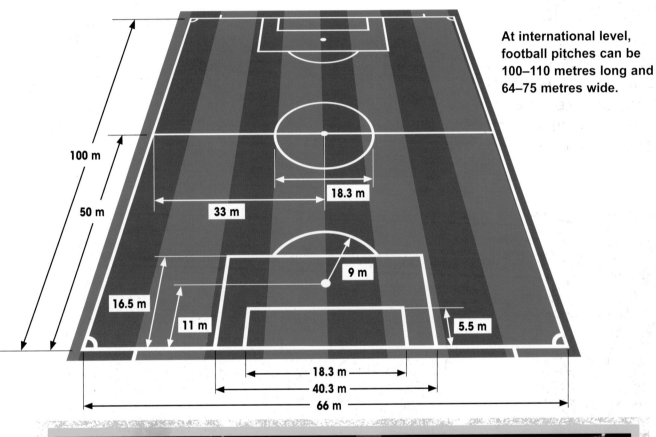

At international level, football pitches can be 100–110 metres long and 64–75 metres wide.

100 m

50 m

18.3 m

33 m

9 m

16.5 m

11 m

5.5 m

18.3 m

40.3 m

66 m

A keeper stretches down on his goal line to collect a ball. In a full-size goal, the two goal posts are 7.32 metres apart and the crossbar is 2.44 metres above the ground.

Start and finish

A full game of football lasts for 90 minutes. It is divided up into two halves, each lasting 45 minutes, with a 15-minute half-time period. At the start of the second half, teams switch halves, changing the end that they defend. In some competitions, if the score is tied at the end of the 90 minutes, two 15-minute periods of extra time are played.

Winning the toss

A game of football starts with the kick-off. This sees one of the teams play the ball from the centre spot in the middle of the pitch, while opposition players stand outside the centre circle (see page 13). Just before the start of a match, the teams will decide which end they will defend and who should take the kick-off. This is usually decided with the toss of a coin by the referee. The team that guesses correctly gets to choose which end to defend or if they want to take the kick-off. Kick-offs are also used to restart a game after a goal has been scored.

The kick-off

1 When teams line up for the kick-off, only players from the team kicking off (in blue) are allowed inside the centre circle. Opposition players (in yellow) must stand outside.

2 One of the players in the team kicking off will take responsibility for the first touch. He must move the ball forwards, otherwise the referee will award a free-kick to the opposition.

3 After the first kick, the second touch must be made by another player. He can pass the ball in any direction.

Open play

After the kick-off, the game continues all over the field. This is called open play. Play carries on until one of the following happens: the ball leaves the pitch and is out of play, a goal is scored, a foul or serious injury occurs, the referee stops play for an unexpected incident, such as a pitch invasion by fans, or the ball is damaged. If the game is stopped with the ball still in open play, the referee restarts the game with a drop ball – dropping the ball between a player from each side. The two players cannot compete for the ball or touch it until it hits the ground.

Towards the end of each half of the match, the fourth official will hold up an electronic sign showing how many minutes are added on to the end of a match due to injuries and other stoppages.

ON THE BALL

At the 1990 World Cup semi-final between Italy and Argentina, referee Michel Vautrot forgot to check the time and accidentally added eight extra minutes of play.

In or out?

Many decisions in football involve officials determining whether the ball was in or out of play. The ball is in play when it is on the pitch, and out of play when it has crossed the lines marking the pitch boundary.

Over the line

In order for a ball to be out of play, it has to cross the lines marking the edge of the pitch completely. If any part of the ball is touching the lines, then it is still in play. This also applies to when a goal is scored. A goal is awarded when the whole of the ball crosses the goal line between the two goal posts. When the ball has gone out of play, the game is restarted by a throw-in if the ball crossed a sideline. If the ball crossed the goal line outside of the goal posts, then the game is restarted with a goal kick if an attacker was the last player to touch the ball. If a defender was the last person to touch the ball, then the attacking team is awarded a corner.

Out of play

In play
If any part of the ball is on the edge of a sideline or goal line, it is still in play.

ON THE BALL

In 2008, Adidas tested a new football with electronic sensors inside. These send data to the referee's watch, telling the referee when the ball is in or out of play.

RULE SCHOOL
You are allowed to score a goal directly from a corner, without the ball touching another player. However, you cannot score directly from a throw-in.

Restarting

There are several laws to follow when taking throw-ins and corners. If a player commits a foul throw (see right), then the opposition is awarded the throw-in. For a corner, the ball must be placed inside a quadrant on the side of the pitch where the ball went out of play. If a player fails to follow the laws regarding taking a corner, then the opposition is awarded a free-kick.

Foul throws

This player has stepped over the sideline with both feet while taking a throw-in. A referee would also award a foul throw if he had stepped over the line with just one foot.

This player has taken one hand off the ball while throwing in. Foul throws are also awarded when the player does not take the ball back behind his head or if he has one foot in the air.

Wesley Sneijder, here playing for Spanish club Real Madrid, prepares to take a corner. A corner-taker can't kick the ball a second time until another player has touched it.

Fouls

There are many different types of fouls in football. A foul may be violent or dangerous play or it could involve holding back a player and stopping them from getting to the ball.

Excessive contact

Football is considered a non-contact sport. In reality, some contact is allowed, but most fouls occur when the referee considers that there has been excessive (too much) contact. These fouls include a player pushing or holding another player, jumping or charging at an opponent, or when a player attempts to make a tackle but makes contact with the opponent before touching the ball. A player is guilty of a foul if they kick or trip an opponent. Even if they attempt but fail to perform these offences, the referee can signal a foul.

Alexandru Gatcan of Moldova (in blue) collides with Luka Modric of Croatia, committing a foul. In some cases, even if a serious foul like this has happened, the referee will wave play on if the team that has been fouled is in a good position. This is called playing advantage.

Other offences

Dangerous play is considered a foul. This is when, for example, a player lifts their foot high to try to kick the ball when it is near an opponent's head. Handball is a foul and occurs when a player deliberately lets an arm or hand connect with the ball. However, when the ball is kicked from one or two metres away straight at an opponent's arm, the referee rarely signals handball. Obstruction is when a player not playing the ball stops an opponent from getting past by blocking their path.

The defender (in yellow) is pulling on the attacker's shirt and holding her back. If the attacker was in the penalty area, then the referee could award the attacker a penalty (see pages 28–29) for being held back from a goal-scoring opportunity.

Misconduct

A number of offences are grouped together and called misconduct. These have to be judged by the referee, who may issue red or yellow cards.

Misconduct

Players are guilty of misconduct if, for example, they deliberately delay the game being restarted. They can do this by holding onto the ball when it should go to the other team or by standing in front of where a free-kick is to be taken and not retreating the required distance. Dissent is refusing to accept a referee's decision or arguing with the match officials. For all of the above offences, a referee is likely to caution the players and show them a yellow card (see pages 22–23).

> **Referees and players have got to trust each other. We are not enemies, we just do our jobs in different ways.**
>
> Italian referee
> **Pierluigi Collina**

Match officials step in to stop players from English clubs Chelsea and Manchester United arguing. In these situations, officials need to act quickly to prevent any violent behaviour.

Álvaro Recoba of Uruguay takes off his shirt while celebrating a goal during a match against Argentina. Such behaviour is a misconduct offence and a referee will show the guilty player a yellow card (see pages 22–23).

Violence, professional fouls and simulation

Footballers sometimes abuse opponents, spectators or the referee, fight, spit at another player or make particularly brutal and dangerous tackles. Such actions break the laws of football and are usually punished heavily. Even when a foul is not particularly brutal, it can result in the player being sent off because they deliberately denied the other team a clear chance to score a goal. This is known as a professional foul. Simulation is pretending to be fouled and hurt, usually to get an opponent in trouble or to win a penalty or free-kick unfairly.

ON THE BALL

During a match at the 2002 World Cup, Brazil's Rivaldo faked being hit in the face by a ball kicked by an opponent. After the match, Rivaldo was fined 11,670 Swiss francs.

Red and yellow

A referee can punish players by showing them a yellow or red card. A yellow card, or booking, cautions a player and warns them about their conduct. A red card indicates that the player has been sent off.

Cautions and sendings off

Cards are awarded by the referee when a player is guilty of a foul or misconduct. If these are serious enough, the referee cautions the player and shows them a yellow card. Two yellow cards in the same match equal a red card. So, if that player commits another serious foul, the referee will show them a second yellow card, followed by a red. When players are shown a red card, they must leave the pitch, and their team has to continue with one player less. If a player is guilty of abusive or violent play, the referee may send them straight off.

Many players will appeal to the referee to try to change a decision. Here, Bastian Schweinsteiger of German club Bayern Munich pleads with the referee not to book one of his team-mates. The pleading failed, as his team-mate was sent off.

Sent to the stands

In many competitions, a record is kept of the red and yellow cards collected by a player. In the 2006 World Cup, any player receiving two yellow cards in matches during the early stages of the competition was banned from playing in the next game. Referees can also show cards to players and coaching staff who are standing on the sidelines. At Euro 2008, referee Manuel Mejuto González sent off both the German manager, Joachim Löw, and the Austrian manager, Josef Hickersberger, for arguing with the fourth official. When a manager is sent off, they have to leave the edge of the pitch, usually to take a seat up in the stadium. A ban from sitting with their team at the side of the pitch for one or more future games usually follows.

A referee books a Vietnamese defender for holding up play by not retreating enough prior to a free-kick being taken in a match against China.

Free-kicks

Free-kicks are awarded by referees for fouls, infringements and misconduct. Teams awarded a free-kick may pass or shoot, while opposition players must stand nine metres away and cannot challenge the first kick.

RULE SCHOOL
Indirect free-kicks are sometimes awarded deep inside an opponent's penalty area. Defenders can stand on the goal line, even if they are less than nine metres away from the free-kick.

Direct and indirect

There are two types of free-kick: direct and indirect. A direct free-kick allows a team to shoot directly on goal with the first kick of the ball. An indirect free-kick requires the ball to be touched once by one player before another player can shoot. Direct free-kicks are awarded when a foul has been committed, such as a trip or push, or for making excessive contact with a player. Indirect free-kicks are awarded for technical offences, such as when a goalkeeper picks up a pass from a team-mate (see page 9). Providing the ball is stationary, teams can take a free-kick quickly, while the opposition players are disorganised, or slowly, so that they can plan what to do.

Three attackers discuss their options for a free-kick close to goal. One of them could shoot directly at the goal, or they could pass the ball to one side for a team-mate to shoot instead.

The defending team

When a free-kick is awarded, the players of the defending team have to retreat nine metres immediately. A defender who kicks the ball away or stands in front of a free-kick taker to stop them taking the kick may be cautioned by the referee. When a free-kick is awarded close to a defending team's goal, the defenders will usually form a wall of three or more players to help protect their goal. The goalkeeper will shout instructions to the players in the wall, telling them exactly where to stand so that they shield part of the goal.

"With a free-kick around the penalty area, we always ask the players whether they want it quick or slow. As long as the ball is stationary and in the right place, then the attacking team can take it as quickly as they like.

Former FIFA referee
Graham Poll

An attacker lines up to shoot a direct free-kick. In front of him, three defenders stand close together to form a wall. This shold be positioned carefully with the help of the goalkeeper, otherwise the free-kick taker may have a clear shot on goal.

Offside!

The offside rule prevents attacking players from waiting around the opposition goal. It is a very difficult law to judge, because referees and assistants need to be aware of where every player on the pitch is standing.

The basic rule

Players are in an offside position if, at the moment the ball is played, they do not have two of the opposing team between themselves and the other team's goal line. A player who is level with two opponents or with the second-from-last opponent is not offside. When a player is signalled offside, the opposing team gets an indirect free-kick from the point where the player was offside.

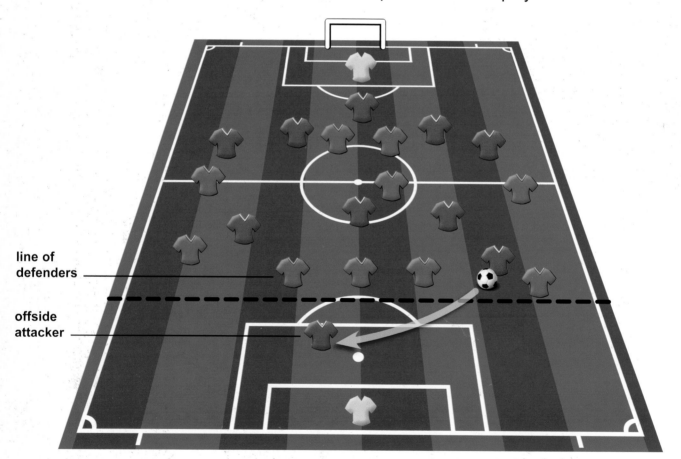

line of defenders

offside attacker

Here, the attacker in red is in an offside position because they are behind the line of defenders when the pass is made. Players are ruled offside only if they are in 'active play', such as drawing a defender or playing the ball.

Exceptions

There are a number of situations where a player may be standing in what looks like an offside position, but the game continues without offside being given. You cannot be offside if you are in possession of the ball, you are in your own half of the pitch or if you receive the ball directly from a throw-in, corner kick or goal kick. This is why an attacker will sometimes sprint towards the opponent's goal after a goal kick. Players can also time their runs so that they are not offside as the ball is kicked, and then run past defenders to collect the ball.

A referee's assistant signals offside by holding out his flag in front of him.

"An offside may only be... an offence when the ball is played by a team-mate... you cannot be judged offside from a pass from the opposition.

Australian referee
Steve Alexander"

Penalties and shootouts

A penalty is a free shot by an attacking player that is taken from the penalty spot. A penalty is a great opportunity to score, because the player who takes the penalty has only the keeper to beat.

Taking a penalty

Penalties are awarded when players in their own penalty area commit a foul or handball for which the referee would normally award a direct free-kick. Only two players are allowed inside the penalty area during a penalty – the goalkeeper and the penalty-taker. The penalty-taker places the ball on the penalty spot, 11 metres from goal, takes a run-up and must kick the ball forwards. If a player from the defending team steps into the penalty area before the kick has been made, the referee can order the kick to be retaken if the penalty is missed.

An attacker (in blue) runs up to take a penalty while a team-mate and defenders wait outside the penalty area. The goalkeeper must stay on the line until the kick has been made, but he can move along the line between the goal posts.

Penalty shootout

A penalty shootout is a series of penalties used to decide the winner of a match that has ended in a draw. Shootouts are usually held at the end of drawn matches in knock-out competitions. Five players from each side take a penalty and, if the scores are still level, penalties continue until one side misses and one scores. The pressures on penalty-takers are immense – one mistake and their team could lose the entire match.

Antonio Puerta (in red) of Spanish side Sevilla scores during a penalty shootout in the 2007 UEFA Cup final against Espanyol of Spain. Sevilla won the shootout and the final 3–1.

> **"** *I am so sorry for missing the penalty and denying the fans, my team-mates, family and friends the chance to be European champions.* **"**
>
> Chelsea captain, **John Terry**, on missing a penalty in the shootout in the 2008 Champions League final against Manchester United

RULE SCHOOL
If a penalty shootout lasts 11 penalties per side without a winner, then every player in a team has to take a penalty, including the goalkeeper.

What it takes to be...

A referee

Pierluigi Collina

The world's most recognisable referee first took a refereeing course at the age of 18. After completing a degree in economics, Collina rose through the refereeing ranks in Italy and began taking charge of matches in the top two divisions, Serie A and Serie B, from 1991 onwards. Considered an outstanding, fair and accurate official, he was promoted to FIFA's list of referees, which enabled him to referee important club and international matches.

Career path

⚽ 1988: Refereeing Italian Serie C1 and C2 matches.

⚽ 1995: Appointed to FIFA's list of referees after just over 40 Serie A matches.

⚽ 1996: Refereed Olympic Games football final.

⚽ 2002: Refereed the final of the FIFA World Cup.

⚽ 2003: Voted world's best referee sixth time in a row.

⚽ 2004: Refereed UEFA Cup final.

⚽ 2010: Appointed chief refereeing officer for UEFA.

Collina stopped refereeing in 2005 when he reached the referees' official retirement age of 45.

Glossary

booking also called a caution, this is when the referee warns a player for dangerous play and shows a yellow card.

corner restarting the game when the ball has gone out of play over the goal line and a defender was the last person to touch the ball.

extra time two periods of 15 minutes each that are added to the end of some matches when they have finished in a draw. Teams swap ends at the end of the first period of extra time.

FIFA (Fédération Internationale de Football Association) the organisation that governs football around the world.

free-kick an uncontested kick awarded to a team after an opposition player commits an offence, such as a foul, dangerous play or a handball.

half-time a short period, usually of 15 minutes, separating two halves of a match.

kick-off restarting the game from the centre spot in the middle of the pitch, used at the start of each half and after a goal.

non-contact sport a sport that does not rely on players physically stopping or blocking opposition players.

open play continuous play until the ball goes out of play or an offence is committed.

throw-in restarting the game after the ball has gone out of play over one of the sidelines. The ball is thrown back onto the pitch by a player using both hands.

toss before the match, the referee tosses a coin and the side that guesses heads or tails correctly chooses whether to take the kick-off or which end to defend.

Books

Sporting Skills: Football by Clive Gifford (Wayland, 2008)
Football: Rules of the Game by Jim Kelman and Philip Morrison (Wayland, 2006)
Inside Sport: Football by Clive Gifford (Wayland, 2007)

Websites

www.footballreferee.org
Website of the Referee's Association that tells you how you can become a referee and the qualifications you will need.

www.fifa.com/worldfootball/ lawsofthegame/index.html
Contains a link so that you can download the latest laws of the game for free.

Index